The Autobiography of
SIR THOMAS BODLEY

The Autobiography of
SIR THOMAS BODLEY

With an Introduction and Notes
by William Clennell

Bodleian Library
UNIVERSITY OF OXFORD

A NOTE ON THE TEXT

The spelling of the 1647 edition printed by Henry Hall has been retained except for initial 'V' and 'VV' which have been modernized as 'U' and 'W'. Paragraph breaks have been added and punctuation has been modernized slightly.

Cover Image: Miniature of Thomas Bodley
By Nicholas Hilliard (1547–1618/19)
Hilliard had known the Bodley family since boyhood, when his father, an Exeter goldsmith, gave him into their care during the European exile. John Bodley was later one of his patrons (**Lane Poole 73**).

First published in 2006 by the Bodleian Library
Broad Street, Oxford, OX1 3BG

www.bodleianbookshop.co.uk

ISBN 1 85124 340 2
ISBN 13 978 85124 340 2

Copyright © Bodleian Library, University of Oxford 2006

Designed by Melanie Gradtke
Printed and bound by L.E.G.O. S.p.A., Vicenza, Italy
A CIP record of this publication is available from the British Library

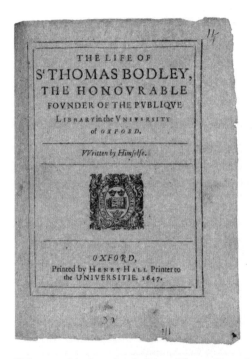

THE LIFE OF
Sᵗ THOMAS BODLEY,
THE HONOVRABLE
FOVNDER OF THE PVBLIQVE
Library in the VNIVERSITY
of OXFORD.

Written by Himselfe.

OXFORD,
Printed by HENRY HALL, Printer to
the UNIVERSITIE. 1647.

Title-page of the first printed edition of the autobiography,
1647. Its publication in June of that year coincides with the
beginning of the University's defensive campaign against the
parliamentary Visitors. Henry Hall had been the printer of
Mercurius Aulicus, 1642–45, the principal royalist newspaper during the Civil War **(Wood 535 (4))**.

CONTENTS

INTRODUCTION

THE *Life of Sir Thomas Bodley*,[1] written in 1609, is primarily of interest as the autobiography of the greatest benefactor of the University of Oxford. It is remarkable for its classical English style, which displays the author's gift for striking phrases, evident not only here but in his official correspondence as a diplomat, and in his letters to the University and to Thomas James, his first Librarian.[2] It has also in recent times been identified as the first English autobiography in which the subject's life is so narrated, within a rhetorical framework, as to constitute an apologia, thus inaugurating a new genre.[3] In this it differs from what appears to be the first continuous autobiographical writing in English, the colourful life story of the composer Thomas Whythorne (*c.*1528–96), written as a narrative connecting a collection of his poems.[4] Bodley's *Life* follows its subject from his early education and academic career, through his involvement in affairs of state, in politics and diplomacy, to the great crisis in which his ambition was frustrated amidst factional strife in the mid 1590s, and to the resolution of that crisis by his momentous decision to re-found the University Library at Oxford.

Self-justification might seem hardly to be required of an author already assured of permanent fame; indeed the brief coda in which he compresses this late stage of his life clearly indicates his awareness of that renown. The aim of the *Life* is by no means the mere self-glorification suggested in the first recorded comment on it. On 10 February 1613, shortly after Bodley's death, John Chamberlain[5] wrote to Sir Ralph Winwood[6] (Bodley's stepson-in-law): 'He hath written his owne life in seven sheetes of paper, and not leaving out the least *minutezze,* or omitting nothing that might tend to his owne glorie or commendation, he hath not so much as made mention of his wife or that he was maried, wherby you may see what a mind he carried, and what account he made of his best benefactours'.[7] But Bodley could take his fame as assured: 'I need not be the publisher of mine owne Institution' (since 1604, by decree of James I, the Library had been known as 'The Library of the Foundation of Sir Thomas Bodley', and since 1605 as *Bibliotheca Bodleiana*). Nevertheless, he evidently felt a need to reclaim his reputation for honour in public life, and to set out the motives underlying both his career in the affairs of state, and the great undertaking which immortalized him.

Why should Bodley have chosen to write his *Life* at this time? In December 1609, he was approaching the end of his life, already suffering from

Sir Thomas Bodley's signature, on the deed ratifying his endowment of the Library, 20 April 1609. This form is consistent with other occurrences of the signature, and with Bodley's fine and very legible italic hand.

the infirmities of age, and was no doubt conscious of the need to leave a personal testament. But it seems possible that, besides intimations of his own mortality, there was a more specific occasion. The autobiography is dated 15 December 1609. Just over a week earlier, on 7 December, Bodley had been one of the chief mourners at the funeral of his neighbour in Parsons Green, Fulham, Sir Thomas Smith,[8] who was also a friend, and a benefactor of the Library. Smith's career had run a course remarkably parallel to Bodley's. He too was an Oxford man who won preferment through the patronage network of the Earl of Leicester, becoming University Orator, and Secretary to the Earl of Essex, a position which involved him in the diplomacy relating to the conflict with Spain. However, by contrast with Bodley, association with Essex during the hostility between his master and Lord Burghley and the Cecil family in the mid-1590s, proved no bar to further advancement, which he gained through Cecilian patronage. Indeed, until his final protracted illness, he seemed destined to accede to the very post of Secretary which had, in this account, eluded Bodley during that difficult period. The ironic contrast with his own life, and that of several other public servants, such as Sir Henry Unton[9] and Bodley's exact contemporary Sir William Russell,[10] whose careers had foundered in those dangerous waters, may well have influenced Bodley's preponderant allocation in the *Life* to the events of 1596. He may also have recalled the earlier setback experienced by Francis Bacon[11] when Essex mounted a campaign to have him elected as attorney-general.[12]

Until that point, the work is very much a summary of a life, with, as Chamberlain pointed out, some omissions from the record. There is for instance, little emphasis, in the account of his early years, on the importance of Calvin's Geneva as a capital of the Reformation, whose influence would spread into that Protestant Europe in which Bodley became a notable public servant.[13] Nor does he mention the eminence in that movement of his own father. John Bodley[14] was a senior in the Geneva congregation, a friend of Miles Coverdale,[15] and an associate of the translators of the 'Geneva Bible' of 1560; indeed he ran the press (earlier used for works of Calvin) on which it was printed, and was later granted a patent to publish it in England. He was an elder of the French protestant church in London, and a treasurer of the fund to raise money for Geneva.

Among John Bodley's acquaintances in the community of English protestant exiles in the reign of Mary Tudor was Laurence Humphrey,[16] the puritan President of Magdalen, the college at which, under Humphrey's tutelage, the fourteen-year old Thomas's Oxford career began. At the age of nineteen, no doubt with the support of Humphrey, Bodley was elected a fellow of Merton College, where, in addition to those duties mentioned in his account, he served several times as Bursar and in other college offices, promoted the study of Hebrew (taught there by his friend John Drusius[17]) and above all established the lifelong friendship with Henry Savile[18] which was to be of such importance in the later stages of his life. Outside the college he held university positions, as Junior Proctor in 1569, and as deputy to the Public Orator.

Bodley's Oxford career effectively ended in September 1576, when he was granted licence to travel abroad by the crown, and was given leave of absence, with an annual stipend of £3.13s.4d., by Merton. He returned after four years, and was senior fellow until, upon his marriage in 1586, he became no longer eligible, but was little seen in Oxford after this point, being engaged in affairs of state. The autobiography omits much of his involvement in court circles, as Gentleman Usher, or Esquire of the Body to the Queen from about 1585, and as a member (though not a notably active one) of the parliaments of 1584 and 1586, in which he sat respectively for Portsmouth and St Germans. His travels abroad, in France and Italy and Germany, included also activity in the intelligence networks of the Earl of Leicester[19] and Sir Francis Walsingham,[20] whom John Chamberlain in another letter, (to Sir Dudley Carleton,[21] 25 February 1613) complaining of their omission from the autobiography, speaks of, with Lady Bodley, as 'all his maine raisers'. Leicester was Chancellor of the University, always on the lookout for Oxford recruits to his service; his secretary was Arthur Atye,[22] Principal of St Alban Hall, and the University Orator for whom Bodley had deputized during his Merton career. The sparse mentions of Bodley in the public records of these years are nevertheless sufficient to indicate his usefulness. In 1579 he is reported to have returned from a visit to Orleans, then a noted centre of Protestantism.[23] And in 1580 the English ambassador to Paris reported that he had been engaged, because of his good acquaintance with the Italian nation, to report on a proposed plot by a mysterious group of confederates led by one Paulo Innocentio.[24] Later, at home, in 1587, he was, with William Waad[25] and others, engaged, on the instruction of the Privy Council, in questioning a suspected spy, by use of the rack if necessary.[26]

During these years Bodley clearly acquired a reputation as a trusted emissary, for he speaks with some pride of being sent on a mission to Denmark and Brunswick in an attempt, which proved unsuccessful, to bring together the King of Denmark with the Duke of Brunswick and other North German protestant princes, into an alliance against Spain. This took place over three months from April 1585.[27] And in the letter written in Elizabeth's own hand which in May 1588 he took unaccompanied to Henri III of France to assure him of her support, he is described as 'confidant et sage et secret'.[28] He does not mention a dramatic dash in 'a good and nimble bark' across the North Sea in August 1588 to persuade the King of Denmark and the merchants of Hamburg not to offer assistance to the Spanish Armada.[29]

However, the most famous omission from the *Life* is that of his marriage. In July 1586 he married

Ann Ball,[30] the wealthy widow of Nicholas Ball, fish-merchant and Mayor of Totnes, who was MP for the borough in the parliament of 1584, in which Bodley represented Portsmouth. A further connection is that Ball was a close business associate of Walter Bogan, who was married to Bodley's sister Prothesia. An ambassador needed private means, and Bodley might also have been encouraged in the marriage by those who wished to advance his diplomatic career. Although it has been said that this fortune enabled Bodley to finance the library, often popularly described as being 'founded on pilchards', it must not be forgotten that he inherited substantially on his father's death in 1591, and that he brought to the management of the fortune an astute ability for investing in property, as shown by the extensive estate which he bequeathed to the University for the endowment and extension of the Library.

The summit of his diplomatic career was the eight years, interrupted by two periods back in

England, which he spent as Elizabeth's ambassador to the Netherlands, as one of the two representatives on the Council of State she was entitled to nominate under the terms of the Treaty of Nonsuch (1585).[31] Bodley took over this position at a time of strain between England and the United Provinces, following the divisive governorship of the Earl of Leicester. He gives a brief summary of his embassy, indicating that a much longer treatise would be required for a full explanation of the reasons for the success of his mission. In fact he had already written a detailed account of his negotiations with the Dutch, in which much more is made of his difficulties with the States General.[32] Bodley's time in the Netherlands was uncomfortable for a number of reasons. Support for the United Provinces' revolt against Spain was a principal part of Elizabeth's foreign policy. Under the Treaty, the Queen had agreed to keep a standing army in the Netherlands, and had made considerable loans. A principal element of Bodley's brief was to persuade the Dutch to support the English troops financially, and to repay the Queen's loans. Bodley held a weak hand in these negotiations. It was at a time when effective power was exercised, not by the nominated Council of State, but by the States General (the delegates of the sovereign provinces, dominated by Holland), and in particular by the *Landsadvocaat* Johan van Oldenbarneveldt,[33] under whose leadership the Provinces gained a new confidence and the beginnings of their rise as a world economic power. Procedural delays and protestations of poverty on the part of the States impeded Bodley's efforts, and it was not until 1598, after his retirement, that a settlement was negotiated, for which however William Camden[34] gives Bodley much credit. He had often asked to be recalled from the mission, and finally was able to return in 1597.

The next and most detailed part of the *Life* is concerned to redeem the author's honour. During his time in the Netherlands he had reported principally to Lord Burghley,[35] the Lord Treasurer, but

Portrait of William Cecil, first Baron Burghley (1520/21–1598), the Lord Treasurer, to whom Bodley reported during his years as English representative in the Netherlands. He is portrayed riding a mule, which was his custom in the walks at his principal residence, Theobalds. The portrait appropriately hangs in the Proscholium entrance to the Bodleian **(Lane Poole 38).**

also maintained a connection with Burghley's great rival, the Earl of Essex, often sending him virtually identical despatches. This association seems natural in the light of Essex's relationship with Leicester (his step-father), and may well also have been encouraged by Henry Savile, who was closely associated with the Earl. It was Essex's recommendation of Bodley for the post of Secretary of State, which incurred the suspicion of Burghley, who had also proposed him at least for a share in that office with his son Robert Cecil,[36] who was in fact appointed to the Secretaryship. The Cecils believed that Bodley was behaving duplicitously, leading to the withdrawal of their support. That is a brief summary of Bodley's case, which is substantially accepted by Camden.[37]

Bodley, who presents himself throughout as a loyal and impartial public servant, now records his distaste for faction (the 'throng of court contentions') and the decision 'to set up my Staffe at the Library doore in Oxford' clearly made before his first letter to the University in February 1598,[38] employing what he knew to be his great abilities in the project which, much more than any political success, has ensured his enduring fame. As Wooden puts it, Bodley 'perceived an essential rhythm that had led him from the study to public service and back to the university' and 'chose to give his autobiography a larger application by casting it as a kind of parable of the Tudor humanist in a fallen world'.[39]

Besides its intention of self-justification, the *Life* is also to be read as an account of preparation for the foundation of the Library. Bodley in one of its many memorable passages, lists 'such foure kinds of aids, as unlesse I had them all, there was no hope of good successe'. These may be summarized as: leisure, learning, money, and friends. With the first he was amply supplied in his 'surcease from the Common-wealth affaires'. Throughout his life he had acquired 'some kind of knowledge, as well in the learned and moderne tongues, as in sundry

Sir Thomas Bodley's Benefactors' Book, 1604. Binding.
A register of donations had been kept in the Library since
1602. In 1604 the entries were printed, in a unique copy (by the
King's Printer, Robert Barker), and when bound, the register
was sent in June of that year for display in the library. It was an
important feature of Sir Thomas's policy of 'stirring up other
men's benevolence' 'Quarta Perennis' appears to be the first oc-
curence of the Founder's motto on his arms, shortly after he
was knighted by James I **(Library Records b. 903, pp.90–91).**

other sorts of scholasticall literature'. He had lec-
tured in Greek; Hebrew, which he had learned first
as a boy, remained a life-long interest; and he was
fluent in the modern languages needed in his diplomatic career, throughout which he maintained his
academic contacts. As has been noted, he is reticent
on the source of his wealth. But the 'very great store
of honourable friends' acquired during his several
careers, forming often intersecting networks, was
perhaps of even greater importance. Benefactors
and advisers are to be found in academia (notably
Sir Henry Savile and many other Oxford academ-
ics); in political and ambassadorial circles (members
of the Privy Council, and ambassadors to Moscow[40]
and Constantinople, and most splendidly the Earl
of Essex, who presented over 250 volumes removed
from the library of the bishop of Faro on his expe-
dition against Cadiz); among the Merchant Ven-
turers trading with Aleppo;[41] and in those members
of the book trade who helped him to conclude the
agreement with the Stationers' Company in 1610[42]

which was one of the most important events in the Library's history, leading to the Bodleian's present status as a library of legal (or copyright) deposit. This is not the place to discuss the formation and early history of the Library, which has been extensively discussed elsewhere, not least in Bodley's wonderful letters to his first Keeper, Thomas James.[43] But this achievement can certainly be seen as the magnificent outcome of the Founder's life as he narrates it.

What was Bodley's intended readership? There is no mention of the *Life* until shortly after his death. John Chamberlain, in his letter to Sir Dudley Carleton of 11 February 1613 bases his account on notes made by Sir Henry Savile while reading it, which implies that it circulated among his friends, and probably, given the number of copies and notes surviving or otherwise recorded, a wider circle. However, in his letter to Sir Ralph Winwood of the day before, Chamberlain states that 'this treatise is commended to the handes of the prime prelate

(George Abbott,[44] archbishop of Canterbury, an
old friend of Bodley and an overseer of his will),
who I feare will suppresse yt, for he hath too much
judgement to let yt be published'. Whether or not
it was intended at that stage to print it, the work is
clearly intended to justify Bodley's life in the eyes
of posterity. One might wonder whether he had in
mind also that, at the very moment of its compo-
sition, William Camden was collecting materials
for his *Annales Rerum Anglicarum et Hibernicarum,
Regnante Elizabetha* (Annals of the reign of Elizabeth), from the archives of his (and Bodley's) late
patron Lord Burghley, from the royal archives, and
from the library of Sir Robert Cotton,[45] another
Bodley friend, and benefactor of the Library. A
copy of notes on the *Life* indeed is found in the
Cottonian manuscripts in the British Library (BL,
MS. Cotton Tit.C.vii.170).

A publisher was eventually found in 1647, when
Henry Hall issued it in Oxford at the University
Press, about 7 June of that year, with a preface at-

tributed by F. Madan[46] to Gerard Langbaine.[47] The
place, date and persons, especially if the attribution
to Langbaine is accepted, are significant. Oxford
had been not only a centre of loyalty to the Royalist
cause during the Civil War, and indeed Charles I's
effective headquarters during almost four years, but
the place of publication of much of the controver-
sial literature, in which theology and politics were
inextricably entwined, that was so fundamental to
the conflict. Henry Hall had played a prominent
role in this, notably as publisher of *Mercurius Aulicus*, the chief royalist newspaper from 1642–45. The
University was now at the beginning of its strug-
gle with the Visitors whom parliament had appointed for the 'correction of abuses'. Langbaine,
as Archivist of the University and custodian of its
privileges, was closely associated with its defence,
and indeed translated into Latin the *Reasons of the
Present Judgment of the University of Oxford*, the case
against submission to the Visitors which had been
approved in convocation on 1 June 1647, and pub-

The Divinity School, 1566.
Drawing by John Bereblocke (fl.1557–1572). One of a series of all the university and college buildings, made for the visit of Queen Elizabeth. The upper room had contained the university library, removed by Edward VI's commissioners some sixteen years earlier. Bereblock, a fellow of Exeter College, was Senior Proctor when Bodley was Junior in 1569 **(Bodleian Library, MS. Bodl. 13, f. 16v)**.

lished, first in London, within a day or two of the new edition of Bodley's *Life*.

The introduction does not overtly recruit Bodley to the Royalist cause. But a contrast is drawn between the present, 'an age so wholly lost to vice', and Bodley's 'Actions with the same integrity set downe, as they were first performed'. His work 'savours not the language of our age, that has the Art to murther with a smile, and fold a curse within a prayer, but speakes the Rhetoricke of that better world, where vertue was the garbe, and truth the complement'. The *Reasons of the Present Judgment*, opposing the 'Negative Oath', similarly speaks of these 'unhappy times' in which a charge may be laid against loyal protestants because 'they may swear one thing in their words and in their own sense mean another'. [48] If, against this background, Bodley is seen to portray himself as an honest man in an age of corruption, the publication of the *Life* may have presented to its contemporary readers the memorial of one who could symbolize the integrity of the University at a time when it was beset by political interference. And the memory of the protection of the Bodleian by general Fairfax when the parliamentary forces took Oxford the previous year, would have reinforced the sense of its Founder's having created 'a Monument freed from the lawes of time and ruine'.

The Autobiography of
SIR THOMAS BODLEY

TO THE READER.

WHEN the Great Restorer of Learning, our Munificent Benefactour, SIR THOMAS BOD-LEY, made the happy Exchange of the troubles of this life, with the Glories of a better; The University, according to the greatnesse of his merits, and their losse, in solemne griefe and sadnesse, attended at his Obsequies. But lest the uncharitable censure of the world should apprehend our thankfulnesse buried in the same grave with him, and cold as his dead ashes, in that we pay no after tribute to so engaging a desert; We bring to the Altar of Eternity that part of him which yet, and ever must survive. A Monument freed from the lawes of time and ruine; Supported with the vigour of that name, which hath a seminall strength within it selfe, to make whole volumes live. But lest the judging and severer eye, viewing the nakednesse of this relation, may thence despise the poornesse of our endeavour. That I may speake the worke above all scorne, above all praise;

it was his Owne. Nor durst we call that draught in question, which felt the hand of so exact a Master; but with awe lookt on it, as on the fabrique of an ancient Temple, where the ruine furthers our Devotion; and gaudy ornaments doe but prophane the sad religion of the place. 'Tis true, it savours not the language of our age, that hath the Art to murther with a smile, and fold a curse within a prayer, but speakes the Rhetoricke of that better world, where vertue was the garbe, and truth the complement. Those actions are of low and empty worth, that can shine onely when the varnish of our words doth gild them over. The true Diamond sparkles in its rocke, and in despight of darknesse makes a day. Here then you shall behold Actions with the same integrity set downe, as they were first perform'd. A History describ'd, as it was liv'd. A Councellour that admitted still Religion to the Cabinet: and in his active aimes had a designe on Heaven. A spirit of that height, that happinesse, as in a private fortune to out-doe the fam'd magnificence of mighty Princes: whil'st his single worke clouds the proud fame of the Ægyptian Library; and shames the tedious growth o'th wealthy Vatican. I know how hard a taske 'twill be to perswade any to copy out from this faire patterne; however we cannot yet so farre despaire of ingenuity, as not to expect even from th'unconcern'd disinteressed Reader, a clear esteeme and just resentment of it. If we gaine but this, we shall in part rest satisfied: In an age so wholly lost to vice, conceiving it a great degree of vertue to confesse the lustre of that good which our perverse endeavours still avoyde.

I was borne at Exeter in Devonshire the second of March, 1544[1] descended both by Father[2] and Mother of worshipfull parentage.[3] By my Fathers side, from an antient Family of Bodley, or Bodleigh of Dunscombe by Crediton; and by my Mother,[4] from Robert Hone Esquire, of Ottery Saint Mary, nine miles from Exeter; my Father in the time of Queen Mary, being noted and knowne to be an enemy to Popery,[5] was so cruelly threatned, and so narrowly observed, by those that maliced his Religion, that for the safeguard of himselfe and my Mother, who was wholly affected as my Father, he knew no way so secure, as to fly into Germany: where after a while he found meanes to call over my Mother, with all his children and family, whom he setled for a time at Wesell in Cleveland, (for there, as then, were many English, which had left their Country for their conscience, and with quietnesse enjoyed their meetings and preachings;) and from thence we removed to the Towne of Franckfort, where was in like sort another English Congregation.[6] Howbeit we made no long tarriance in either of those two Townes, for that my Father had resolved to fixe his abode in the City of Geneva,[7] where, as farre as I remember, the English Church consisted of some hundred persons.[8]

I was at that time of twelve years age, but through my Fathers cost and care, sufficiently instructed to become an Auditour of Chevalerius[9] in Hebrew, of Berealdus[10] in Greeke, of Calvin[11] and Beza[12] in Divinity, and of some other Professours in that University; (which was newly then erected[13]) besides my domesticall teachers, in the house of Philibertus Saracenus,[14] a famous Physitian in that City, with whom I was boarded: where Robertus Constantinus,[15] that made the Greeke Lexicon, read Homer unto me.

Thus I remained there two yeares and more, until such time as our Nation was advertised of the death of Queene Mary, & succession of Elizabeth, with the change of Religion, which caused my Father to hasten into England, where he came with

my Mother, and with all their family, within the
first of the Queene, and setled their dwelling in the
City of London.

It was not long after, that I was sent away from
thence to the University of Oxford, recommended
to the teaching and tuition of Doctour Humfrey,[16]
who was shortly after chosen the chiefe Reader
in Divinity, and President of Magdalen Colledge;
there I followed my studies till I tooke the degree
of Batchelour of Arts, which was in the yeare, 1563,
within which yeare I was also chosen Probationer
of Merton Colledge, and the next yeare ensuing
admitted Fellow. Afterwards, to wit in the yeare,
1565, by speciall perswasion of some of my fel-
lowes, and for my private exercise, I undertooke the
publique reading of a Greeke lecture, in the same
Colledge Hall, without requiring or expecting any
stipend for it; Neverthelesse it pleased the Fellow-
ship of their owne accord to allow me soone after
four markes by the yeare, and ever since to continue
that Lecture to the Colledge.[17] In the yeare of our

Lord 1566, I proceeded Master of Arts, and read for
that yeare in the Schoole-streets Naturall Philoso-
phy; after which time, within lesse then three yeares
space, I was wonne by intreaty of my best affected
friends, to stand for the Proctourship, to which I
and my Colleague, Master Bearblocke of Exeter
Colledge, were quietly elected in the yeare 1569,
without any competition or countersuite of any
other.[18] After this for a long time, I supplyed the
office of the University Oratour,[19] and bestowed my
time in the study of sundry faculties, without any
inclination to professe any one aboue the rest, insomuch as at last I waxed desirous to travell beyond
the Seas, for attaining to the knowledge of some
speciall moderne tongues, and for the encrease of
my experience in the managing of affaires, being
wholly then addicted to employ my selfe, and all my
cares, in the publique service of the State.[20]

My resolution fully taken I departed out of
England Anno 1576 and continued very near foure
yeares abroad, and that in sundry parts of Italy,

France, and Germany. A good while after my returne, to wit, in the yeare 1585, I was employed by
the Queene to Fredericke[21] Father to the present
King of Denmarke, to Iulius Duke of Brunswicke,[22]
to William Lantgrave of Hesse,[23] and other German Princes: the effect of my message was, to draw
them to joine their forces with hers, for giving assistance to the King of Navarre now Henry the
fourth King of France.[24]

My next employment was to Henry the third,[25]
at such time as he was forced by the Duke of Guise[26]
to fly out of Paris; which I performed in such sort, as
I had in charge with extraordinary secrecy: not being accompanied with any one servant (for so much
was I commanded) nor with any other Letters, then
such as were written in the Queenes own hand,[27]
to the King, and some selected persons about him;
the effect of that message it is fit I should conceale.
But it tended greatly to the advantage, not only of
the King, but of all the Protestants in France, & to
the Dukes apparent overthrow, which also followed

soon upon it. It so befell after this, in the year 88. that for the better conduct of her Highnesse affaires in the Provinces united, I was thought a fit person to reside in those parts, and was sent thereupon to the Hague in Holland, where according to the contract that had formerly past, betweene her Highnesse and the States,[28] I was admitted for one of their Councell of Estate,[29] taking place in their Assemblies next to Count Maurice,[30] and yeilding my suffrage in all that was proposed.

During all that time what approbation was given of my painefull endeavours by the Queene, Lords in England, by the States of the Country there, and by all the English Souldiery, I referre it to be notified by some others relation; sith it was not unknowne to any of any calling, that then were acquainted with the State of that government. For at my first comming thither, the people of that Country stood in dangerous termes of discontentment, partly for some courses that were held in England, as they thought, to their singular prejudice, but most of all in respect of the insolent demeanour of some of her Highnesse Ministers, which onely respected their private emolument, little weighing in their dealing what the Queene had contracted with the States of the Country; whereupon was conceived a mighty feare on every side, that both a present dissolution of the Contract would ensue, and a downright breach of amity betweene us and them.

Now what meanes I set a foot for redresse of those perils, and by what degrees the state of things was reducd into order, it would require a long treatise to report it exactly,[31] but this I may averre with modesty and truth, and the Country did alwaies acknowledge it with gratitude, that had I not of my selfe, without any direction from my Superiours, proceeded in my charge with extreame circumspection, as well in all my speeches and proposalls to the States, as in the tenour of my letters that I writ into England, some suddaine alarme had beene given, to the utter subversion and ruine of the State of those Provinces: which in processe of time must needs have wrought in all probability, the self-same effect in the state of this Realme.

Of this my diligence and care in the managing of my business, there was, as I have signified, very speciall notice taken by the Queene and State at home, for which I received from her Majesty many comfortable Letters of her gracious acceptance: as withall from that time forward I did never receive allmost any set instructions how to governe my proceedings in her Majesties occasions, but the carriage in a manner of all her affaires was left to mee and my direction.

Through this my long absence out of England, which wanted very little of five whole yeares, my private estate did greatly require my speedy returne, which when I had obtained by intercession of friends, and a tedious suite, I could enjoy but a while, being shortly after enjoyned to repaire to the Hague againe. Neverthelesse upon a certain occasion to deliver unto her some secret overtures, and of performing thereupon an extraordinary service,

I came againe home within lesse than a Twelve-moneth: and I was no sooner come, but her High-nesse embracing the fruit of my discoveries, I was presently commanded to returne to the States with charge to pursue those affaires to performance, which I had secretly proposed; and according to the project which I had conceived, and imparted unto her, all things were concluded and brought to that issue that was instantly desired, whereupon I procured my last revocation.[32]

Now here I can not choose but in making report of the principall accidents that have fallen unto me in the course of my life, but record among the rest, that from the very first day I had no man more to friend among the Lords of the Councell, then was the Lord Treasurer Burleigh:[33] for when occasion had beene offered of declaring his conceit as touching my service, he would alwaies tell the Queene (which I received from her selfe and some other ear-witnesses) that there was not any man in England so meet as my selfe to undergoe the office of the

Secretary.[34] And sithence his sonne,[35] the present Lord Treasurer, hath signified unto me in private conference, that when his father first intended to advance him to that place, his purpose was withall to make me his Colleague.

But the case stood thus in my behalf: before such time as I returned from the Provinces united, which was in the yeare 1597, and likewise after my returne, the then Earle of Essex[36] did use mee so kindly both by letters and messages, and other great tokens of his inward favours to me, that although I had no meaning, but to settle in my mind the cheifest desire and dependance upon the Lord Burleigh, as one that I reputed to be both the best able, and therewithall the most willing to worke my advancement with the Queene, yet I know not how, the Earle, who sought by all devises to divert her love and liking both from the Father and the Son (but from the Sonne in speciall) to withdraw my affection from the one and the other, and to winne mee altogether to depend upon himselfe, did so often take occasion to entertaine the Queene with some prodigall speeches of my sufficiency for a Secretary, which were ever accompanied with words of disgrace against the present Lord Treasurer, as neither she her selfe, of whose favour before I was throughly assured, tooke any great pleasure to preferre me the sooner, (for she hated his ambition, and would give little countenance to any of his followers) and both the Lord Burleigh and his Sonne waxed jealous of my courses, as if under hand I had beene induced by the cunning and kindnesse of the Earle of Essex, to oppose my selfe against their dealings. And though in very truth they had no solid ground at all of the least alteration in my disposition towards either of them both, (for I did greatly respect their persons and places, with a setled resolution to doe them any service, as also in my heart I detested to be held of any faction whatsoever) yet the now Lord Treasurer, upon occasion of some talke, that I have since had with him, of the Earle and his actions, hath freely confessed of his owne accord unto me, that his daily provocations were so bitter and sharpe against him, and his comparisons so odious, when he put us in a ballance, as he thought thereupon he had very great reason to use his best meanes, to put any man out of hope of raising his fortune, whom the Earle with such violence, to his extreame prejudice, had endeavoured to dignifie. And this, as he affirmed, was all the motive he had to set himselfe against me, in whatsoever might redound to the bettering of my estate, or increasing of my credit and countenance with the Queene.

When I had throughly now bethought me, first in the Earle, of the slender hold-fast that he had in the favour of the Queene, of an endlesse opposition of the cheifest of our States-men like still to waite upon him, of his perilloous, and feeble, and uncertain advice, aswell in his owne, as in all the causes of his friends: and when moreover for my selfe I had fully considered how very untowardly these two Counsellours were affected unto me, (upon whom before in cogitation I had framed all the fabrique of my future prosperity) how ill it did concurre with my naturall disposition, to become, or to be counted either a stickler[37] or partaker in any publique faction, how well I was able, by God's good blessing, to live of my selfe, if I could be content with a competent livelyhood, how short time of further life I was then to expect by the common course of nature: when I had, I say, in this manner represented to my thoughts my particular estate, together with the Earles, I resolved thereupon to possesse my soule in peace all the residue of my daies, to take my full farewell of State imployments, to satisfie my mind with that mediocrity of worldly living that I had of my owne, and so to retire me from the Court, which was the epilogue and end of all my actions and endeavours of any important note, till I came to the age of fifty three.

Now although after this, by her Majestie's direction, I was often called to the Court, by the now Lord Treasurer,[38] then Secretary, and required by him, as also divers times since, by order from the

King, to serve as Embassadour in France; to goe a Commissioner from his Highnesse, for concluding the truce between Spaine and the Provinces, and to negotiate in other very honourable imployments, yet I would not be removed from my former finall resolution, insomuch as at length, to induce me the sooner to returne to the Court, I had an offer made me by the present Lord Treasurer (for in processe of time he saw, as he himselfe was pleased to tell me more than once, that all my dealing was upright, faithfull, and direct) that in case I my selfe were willing unto it, he would make me his associate in the Secretaries office; And to the intent I might be-lieve that he intended it Bonâ fide, he would get me out of hand to be sworne of the Counsell. And for the better enabling of my state to maintaine such a dignity, whatsoever I would aske, that might be fit for him to deale in, and for me to enjoy, he would presently sollicite the King to give it passage. All which perswasions notwithstanding, albeit I was of-ten assaulted by him, in regard of my yeares, and for that I felt my selfe subject to many indispositions, besides some other private reasons which I reserve unto my selfe, I have continued still at home, my retired course of life, which is now methinks to me as the greatest preferment that the State can afford. Onely this I must truly confesse of my selfe, that though I did never repent me yet of those and some other my often refusals of honourable offers, in respect of enriching my private estate, yet somewhat more of late I have blamed my selfe, & my nicety that way, for the love that I beare to my Reverend Mother the University of Oxford, and to the advancement of her good, by such kind of means as I have since undertaken. For thus I fell to discourse and debate in my mind, that although I might find it fittest for me, to keep out of the throng of Court contentions, & addresse my thoughts & deeds to such ends altogether, as I my selfe could best affect; yet withal I was to think, that my duty towards God, the expectation of the world, my naturall inclination, & very morality, did require, that I should not wholly so hide those little abilities that I had, but that in some measure, in one kind or other, I should doe the true part of a profitable member in the State: whereupon examining exactly for the rest of my life, what course I might take, and having sought (as I thought, all the waies to the wood) to select the most proper, I concluded at the last to set up my Staffe at the Library doore in Oxford; being throughly perswaded, that in my solitude and surcease from the Common-wealth affaires, I could not busy my selfe to better purpose, then by reducing that place (which then in every part lay ruined and wast) to the publique use of Students;[39] For the effecting whereof, I found myself furnished in a competent proportion, of such foure kinds of aides, as unlesse I had them all, there was no hope of good successe. For without some kinde of knowledge, as well in the learned and moderne tongues, as in sundry other sorts of scholasticall literature,[40] without some purse-ability to goe through with the charge,[41] without very great store of honourable friends to further the designe,[42] and without speciall good leisure to follow such a worke, it could but have proved a vaine attempt, and inconsiderate. But how well I have sped in all my endeavours, and how full provision I have made for the benefit and ease of all frequenters of the Library, that which I have already performed in sight, that besides which I have given for the maintenance of it,[43] and that which hereafter I purpose to adde, by way of en-largement[44] to that place (for the project is cast, and whether I live or dye it shall be, God willing, put in full execution) will testifie so truly and aboundantly for me, as I need not be the publisher of the dignity and worth of mine owne Institution. Written with my owne hand Anno 1609. December the 15.

THO: BODLEY.

Thus farre our Noble Author of himselfe. Who like to the first Pen-man of the sacred history, seemes to survive his grave, and to describe unto us his owne death. For having finished that great worke which future times shall ever honour, never equall, he yielded to his fate, As being unwilling the glory of that deed should be deflour'd by the succession of an act lesse high then it. On the 29th of Ianuary in the yeare 1612 his pure Soule attain'd the freedome of its owne divinity: leaving his borrow'd earth, the sad remainder of innocence and frailty, to be deposited in Merton Colledge: Who had the happinesse to call his Education hers, and to be intrusted with so deare a Pledge of immortality.

FINIS.

NOTES TO THE INTRODUCTION

1   The original manuscript seems not to have survived. The work is preserved in a copy made about 1615, bound in a collection of documents collected by Thomas James relating to the early history of the Library (Bodleian Library, MS. Arch. Selden. A. 76), and in another apparently contemporary copy in a volume also containing a copy of Bodley's will (Bodleian Library, MS. Add. A. 186).

2   G. W. Wheeler (ed.), *The Letters of Sir Thomas Bodley to the University of Oxford* (Oxford, 1927); G. W. Wheeler (ed.), *The Letters of Sir Thomas Bodley to Thomas James, the First Keeper of the Bodleian Library* (Oxford, 1926).

3   W. W. Wooden, 'Sir Thomas Bodley's Life of Himself (1609) and the Epideictic Strategies of Encomia', *Studies in Philology*, 83 (1986), 62–75. See also P. Delany, *British Autobiography in the Seventeenth Century* (London, 1969).

4   Bodleian Library, MS. Eng. misc. c. 330. Published as J. M. Osborne (ed.), *The autobiography of Thomas Whythorne* (Oxford, 1961).

5   John Chamberlain (1553–1628). Chiefly known for the correspondence in which he gives a 'many-sided view of Elizabethan and Jacobean London and England' *(Oxford Dictionary of National Biography* (Oxford, 2004)).

6   Sir Ralph Winwood (1562/3–1617). The King's representative in the Netherlands, 1603–9. Married Bodley's step-daughter, Elizabeth Ball, 1603. Secretary of State, 1614.

7   N. E. McClure (ed.), *The Letters of John Chamberlain*, 2 vols. (Philadelphia, 1939).

8   Sir Thomas Smith (*c.*1556–1609). University Orator 1582–94; Secretary to the Earl of Essex, 1589–. See letter from Sir Thomas Edmondes to William Trumbull, 20 December 1609. Historical Manuscripts Commission, *Report on the Manuscripts of the Marquess of Downshire,* ii (London, 1924), 199. I am most grateful to Bridget Walter of the Bodleian for pointing out this coincidence, as well as for other help with this introduction.

9   Sir Henry Unton (*c.*1558–96). Like Bodley went on a European tour c.1575. Ambassador to France, 1591–2 and 1595.

10 Sir William Russell (*c.*1553–1613). Like Bodley a pupil of Laurence Humphrey at Magdalen. Served under Leicester in the Netherlands. Lord Deputy of Ireland, 1594–7.

11 Francis Bacon, Viscount St Alban (1561–1626). Essex's campaign for his appointment as attorney-general was set up in 1592.

12 For a general discussion of the Essex/Cecil confrontations in this context see P. E. J. Hammer, *The Polarisation of Elizabethan Politics: the Political Career of Robert Devereux, 2nd Earl of Essex* (Cambridge, 1991), 196.

13 See D. J. B. Trim, 'Sir Thomas Bodley and the International Protestant Cause', *Bodleian Library Record*, 16/4 (1998), 314–340.

14 John Bodley (c.1520–1591) a wealthy Exeter merchant, was a principal financier of the relief of the siege of Exeter. He arrived in Geneva with his wife, four children, and three servants in May 1557. Co-signatory with Knox, Coverdale and others of the letter from Geneva to the other English exile congregations urging unity before their return from exile. See F. Rose-Troup, *Biography of John Bodley* (Ottery St Mary, 1903), and Sir *Thomas Bodley, Father and Kindred* (Ottery St Mary, 1903, also *Oxford Dictionary of National Biography*.

15 Miles Coverdale (1488–1569). First translator of the entire Bible into English, 1535. Chaplain to Lord Russell during the siege of Exeter. Bishop of Exeter 1551–3. It has been suggested that John Bodley travelled with him to exile in Germany in 1555.

16 Laurence Humphrey (1525–1589). President of Magdalen, 1561–89. Regius Professor of Divinity, 1560–89.

17 John Drusius (Jan van den Driesche, 1550–1616). Like Bodley a pupil of Chevallier. BA Merton 1572. Professor of Hebrew at Leyden 1577–85, at Franeker 1585–1603. Dedicated to Bodley, as legate to the Council of State, his *Apophthègmata Ebræorum ac Arabum* (Franeker, 1591). In the lengthy dedication he discusses that very edition of the Pirke Avoth, by P. Fagius, which is the probable source of Bodley's motto *Quarta Perennis*. See C. Roth 'Sir Thomas Bodley – Hebraist', *Bodleian Library Record,* 7/5 (1962–67), 242–251.

18 Sir Henry Savile (1549–1622). Warden of Merton and Provost of Eton. A classical scholar, translator of Tacitus , editor of St John Chrysostom and one of the translators of the King James Bible, he was also a scientist, lecturing notably on Copernicus. A close personal friend of Bodley, whom he advised on the design of the Library, which he continued after Bodley's death. Founded, 1619, the Savilian chairs of Geometry and Astronomy.

19 Robert Dudley, Earl of Leicester (1532/3–1588).

20 Sir Francis Walsingham (c.1532–1590). Principal Secretary.

21 Dudley Carleton, Viscount Dorchester (1574–1632). Diplomat, engaged in various missions to France and the Netherlands; ambassador to Venice. Pupil of William Camden at Westminster. Stepson-in-law of Sir Henry Savile.

22 Sir Arthur Atye (c.1540–1603). Student of Christ Church, Fellow of Merton 1562. Principal of St Alban Hall 1569–72. Proctor 1570. Public Orator 1572–82. Private secretary to Earl of Leicester.

23 *Calendar of State Papers Foreign* (London, 1904), 79.

24 *Calendar of State Papers Foreign* (London, 1904), 354–5.

25 William Waad (1546–1623). Servant of Burghley and expert linguist. Diplomatic agent 1576–87. MP for Aldbrough in the Parliament of 1584.

26 *Acts of the Privy Council of England* (London, 1897), 365.

27 Extensively reported in *Calendar of State Papers Foreign,* August 1584–August 1587 (London, 1916), 453, 508ff.

28 *Calendar of State Papers Foreign,* June 1586–June 1588 (London, 1927), 611, 636–7.

29 *Acts of the Privy Council of England,* 1588 (London, 1897), 225, 229.

30 Ann Ball (*c.*1560–1611). Daughter of Richard Cary or Carew, a merchant and Mayor of Bristol. Although he does not mention her here, a touching monument placed by Sir Thomas in the church of St Bartholomew the Less in the city of London records twenty-four years of happy married life ('cum qua feliciter vixit ANN XXIIII'). She is often referred to in Bodley's letters to Thomas James.

31 The other was George Gilpin (d.1602), an experienced diplomat whose command of Dutch (he had long been resident in the Netherlands) was of great assistance to Bodley.

32 Bodleian Library, MS. Bodl. 11. This was printed by Hearne as an appendix to vol.3 of his edition of Camden's *Annales Rerum Anglicarum et Hibernicarum, Regnante Elizabetha.* 1717.

33 Johan van Oldenbarnevelt (1547–1619). His position as *Landsadvocaat* 1586 brought him into conflict with Leicester, and he continued to represent Dutch interests in relation to the English. Bodley speaks of the domination of the States by Oldenbarnevelt 'by whom they are strangely ruled and overruled'. Calendar of State Papers Foreign, January–July 1589, p.51.

34 William Camden, *Tomus Alter Annalium Rerum Anglicarum et Hibernicarum, Regnante Elizabetha.* (London,1627), 165.

35 William Cecil, first Baron Burghley (1520/21–1598).Secretary of State, Lord Treasurer.

36 Robert Cecil, first Earl of Salisbury (1563–1612). Appointed Secretary of State 5 July 1596.

37 Camden, *Tomus Alter Annalium,* 123.

38 His letters of 23 February and 19 March show that a great deal of advance planning with Henry Savile for the supply of timber, and eventual endowments for the Library had already been made. See Wheeler, *Letters of Sir Thomas Bodley to the University of Oxford.*

39 Wooden, 'Sir Thomas Bodley's Life of Himself', 65.

40 Sir Richard Lee (c.1548–1618) Ambassador to Moscow, was present at the opening of the Library and gave, together with Russian material, works in Finnish, and the first example of Chinese to arrive in the Library.

41 Sir Paul Pindar (1565/6–1650). Ambassador to Constantinople and Consul of the English Merchants at Aleppo, at Bodley's request, presented twenty Arabic and Persian manuscripts.

42 Notably John Norton (1556/7–1612). Bodley's first bookseller, and an early benefactor. Master of the Stationers' Company, 1607–8 and 1611–12.

43 Wheeler, *The Letters of Sir Thomas Bodley to Thomas James*. See also W. D. Macray, *Annals of the Bodleian Library* (2nd edn., Oxford, 1890); I. G. Philip, *The Bodleian Library in the Seventeenth and Eighteenth Centuries* (Lyle lectures, 1980-81) (Oxford, 1983).

44 George Abbot (1562–1633). Master of University College Oxford, 1597. Vice-chancellor 1601-6. Bishop of Lichfield 1609. Archbishop of Canterbury 1611–. Bodley several times mentions dining with him in his letters to Thomas James.

45 Sir Robert Bruce Cotton, first baronet (1571–1631). Taught by William Camden at Westminster School. Member of the Society of Antiquaries. His library, a quasi-public institution, was a major source for learned research. He knew Bodley and gave eleven important manuscripts to the Library.

46 F. Madan, *Oxford Books,* ii (Oxford, 1912).

47 Gerard Langbaine (1608/9–1658). University Archivist 1644. Provost of Queen's 1646. Catalogued Greek manuscripts in the Bodleian and initiated a scheme to provide a subject catalogue of the Library.

48 *Reasons Of the present judgment of the University of Oxford, concerning The Solemne League and Covenant* [&c.] (Oxford, 1647), 4, 23.

NOTES TO THE AUTOBIOGRAPHY

1   1545 N.S.

2   John Bodley (c.1520–1591). Religious radical and publisher. See F. Rose-Troup, *Biography of John Bodley* (Ottery St Mary, 1903), and *Oxford Dictionary of National Biography* (Oxford, 2004).

3   For the pedigree of Sir Thomas see F. Rose-Troup, *Sir Thomas Bodley's Father and Kindred* (Ottery St Mary, 1903).

4   Joan Hone, one of the five richly dowered daughters of Robert Hone, a serge merchant and landowner.

5   John Bodley was one of the Exeter merchants who raised money to employ mercenaries for the relief of the siege of Exeter during the 'Rising in the West' against the imposition of the Book of Common Prayer in 1549. See F. Rose-Troup, *The Western Rebellion of 1549* (London, 1913).

6   The English congregation at Frankfurt was much troubled by divisions over ritual and the Prayer Book, and the more purist faction, led by John Knox, removed to Geneva. See T. Wood, *A Brieff Discourse of the Troubles Begonne at Franckford* (Heidelberg, 1574).

7   The Bodley family arrived in Geneva on 10 May 1557.

8   Over 160, including wives and numerous children. See J. S. Burn (ed.), *Livre des Anglois, à Genève* (London, 1831).

9 Anthony Rudolph Chevallier (1523–1572) who later deputized for the Regius Professor of Hebrew at Cambridge. He was probably Princess Elizabeth's French tutor.

10 François Bérauld, not Bérault (fl. 1549–92). Professor of Greek at Lausanne; followed Beza to Geneva in 1559.

11 Jean Calvin (1509–1564). French reformer.

12 Théodore de Bèze (1519–1605). Successor of Calvin in control of Genevan Reformation.

13 The Académie (later Université) de Genève was formally inaugurated in June 1559.

14 Philibert Sarrasin (d.1573). Having previously been a schoolmaster in Agen, and a physician in Lyon, he arrived in Geneva in 1550. His skill as a teacher is attested by the fact that his daughter Louise is said to have been able to read Latin, Greek and Hebrew by the age of eight.

15 Robert Constantin (c.1530–1605). His *Lexicon* was published at Geneva in 1562.

16 Laurence Humphrey (c.1526–1605). Also an exile in Switzerland during Mary's reign; leader of the 'antivestarians' in Oxford; Regius Professor of Divinity, 1560–89; President of Magdalen, 1561–89; Vice-Chancellor, 1571–6. 'He did … stock his college with a generation of nonconformists which could not be rooted out in many years after his decease.' A. Wood. see P. Bliss (ed.), *Athenae Oxoniensis* (London, 1813–20)ii, 559.

17 See J. M. Fletcher (ed.), *Annalium Collegii Mertonensis* 1521–1567 (Oxford, 1974), i. 251.

18 At this time, the Proctors were elected by the Chancellor and Vice-Chancellor, the heads of houses and doctors. John Bereblock (fl.1557–1572) at this time fellow of Exeter College, is chiefly known for the volume containing drawings of all the university and college buildings which was presented to Queen Elizabeth on her visit in 1566. That of the 'Schola Theologiae' is the basis of the modern device or 'logo' of the Bodleian. He was the Senior, Bodley the Junior Proctor.

19 That is, he deputized for Arthur Atye (d.1604) fellow of Merton and Principal of St Alban's Hall, who later, as secretary to the Earl of Leicester, was an influential figure in the political and diplomatic circles in which Bodley moved.

20 Like many members of both universities, Bodley was recruited to the foreign service by influence of the Earl of Leicester, Chancellor of the University at this time. For evidence of his travels abroad see Introduction.

21 Frederick II (1534–1588).

22 Julius, Duke of Brunswick (1528–1589). Conservative in his foreign policy, he was unwilling to join in an alliance against Spain.

23 William IV, Landgrave of Hesse (1532–1592).

24 Henri IV, King of France (1553–1610). For Bodley's contemporary account of this mission see *Calendar of State Papers Foreign*, August 1584–August 1585 (London, 1916), 453, 508ff.

25 Henry III, King of France (1551–1589).

26 Henri Guise-Lorraine, Prince de Joinville and third duc de Guise (1550–1588). This was the episode known as the Jour des Barricades (12 May 1588) when Henry retreated to Blois where Guise was assassinated on 23 December 1588.

27 In the Queen's letter Bodley is described as 'confidant et sage et secret'. *Calendar of State Papers Foreign*, June 1586–June 1588 (London, 1927) 611.

28 The Treaty of Nonsuch, 1585.

29 Raad van State. Elizabeth was entitled by the treaty to appoint two representatives. The other was the bilingual George Gilpin (d.1602).

30 Maurits, Prins van Oranje-Nassau (1567–1625).

31 Bodley in fact wrote a detailed account of these negotiations, preserved in Bodleian Library, MS. Bodl. 11. It was printed as an appendix to the third volume of Thomas Hearne's edition of W. Camden, *Annales Rerum Anglicarum et Hibernicarum, Regnante Elizabetha* (London, 1717).

32 A detailed account of Bodley's mission to the Netherlands (yet to be written) from the National Archives and other collections, would show Bodley as a conscientious and active ambassador, not merely in matters of high policy, in which his pragmatic attitudes towards the Dutch are notable (on more than one occasion incurring the wrath of Elizabeth), but also in the day to day concerns of an ambassador: visiting the sites of bat-

tles, looking after the interests of English merchants and sailors, gathering intelligence and intercepting correspondence from other agents.

33 William Cecil, first Baron Burghley (1520–1598). Secretary of State, Lord Treasurer. The most powerful of Elizabeth's servants.

34 For discussion of this key passage in the Life, see Introduction, and P. Hammer, *The Polarisation of Elizabethan Politics; the Political Career of Robert Devereux, 2nd Earl of Essex, 1585-1597* (Cambridge, 1999).

35 Robert Cecil, first earl of Salisbury (1563–1612). Appointed Secretary of State on 5 July 1596.

36 Robert Devereux, second Earl of Essex. (1565–1601). The great rival for power of the Cecils. Bodley had been an associate and correspondent of Essex during the latter period of his ambassadorship.

37 A moderator or umpire at a tournament , a wrestling match etc., appointed to see fair play and to part the combatants when they have fought enough; one who takes an active or busy part (in contests etc.); a factious, seditious or pragmatic contender *(Oxford English Dictionary).*

38 Robert Cecil, now Earl of Salisbury, was appointed Lord Treasurer in 1608.

39 He wrote to the Vice-Chancellor on 23 February 1598 offering to 'reduce it again to his former use'. See G. W. Wheeler (ed.),

Letters of Sir Thomas Bodley to the University of Oxford (Oxford, 1927), 4.

40 Bodley's interest in Hebrew and other languages continued throughout his public career, as did his academic contacts. See note on John Drusius in introduction n. 17.

41 For Bodley's fortune, see Introduction, on Ann Ball, n. 30.

42 On the intersecting networks of Bodley's friends, see Introduction, and notes 40–42.

43 A note to the Vice-Chancellor of 1609 gives details of 'the many landes and tenements that I have conveyed unto the Universitie'. Wheeler, *Letters to the University of Oxford,* 20.

44 In the same note he writes of property, including the Manor of Hindon, Maidenhead which will 'after my decease to [come] and remain to their use'. He was already planning the extension now known as Arts End, built 1610–12, and had in mind the extension into the Schools Quadrangle which completed the Library as he intended it.

EDITIONS OF
THE LIFE OF SIR THOMAS BODLEY

Manuscripts:

The autograph manuscript, dated 13 December 1609, is stated by Antony Wood (P. Bliss (ed.), *Athenae Oxonienses* (London, 1815) ii, 126.) to be 'kept as a great rarity in the archives of his Library'. This manuscript, from which the first printed edition is presumed to have been made, seems to have disappeared.

A copy, *c.*1615 (in a collection of documents relating to the early history of the Library, in a notebook owned by Thomas James) is in Bodleian Library, MS. Arch. Seld. A. 75.

A contemporary copy, in a volume containing also a copy of Bodley's will and codicil, is stated by the *Summary Catalogue* to be the version printed by Hearne in his *Reliquiæ Bodleianæ* in 1703. Bodleian Library, MS. Add. A. 186.

A copy written about 1630. Followed by 'the uses assigned by Sr. Tho: Bodley in his Tripartite Indenture'. Bodleian Library, MS. Eng. hist. d. 92, ff.63–69.

A manuscript, said to be in Bodley's hand, is stated by J. Prince (see below) to have been in the possession of Walter Bogan of Gatscombe.

Notes made by Sir Henry Savile seen by J. Chamberlain in January 1613.

Notes in British Library, Tit. C. vii. 170. MS. Cotton.

Latin Translations:

Bodleian Library, MS. Smith. 31, 60–68. 'From a paper belonging to Archbishop Ussher.'

Bodleian Library, MS. Add. 379. Ussher Manuscripts, ff.119–123.

Printed versions:

The Life of Sr Thomas Bodley, the Honourable Founder of the Publique Library in the University of Oxford (Oxford, printed by Henry Hall, Printer to the Universitie, 1647).

John Prince, *Danmonii orientales illustres;* or *The Worthies of Devon* (Exeter 1701). Transcript 'from a manuscript (on probable grounds supposed to be in his own Hand-writing) now in the custody of a Neighbour-Gentleman nearly related to his family. Marginal note identifies him as Walter Bogan of Gatscombe Esq (the great grandson of Bodley's sister Prothesia).

T. Hearne (ed.), *Reliquiæ Bodleianæ; or some genuine remains of Sir Thomas Bodley* (London, 1703) 1–15. Transcr. from Bodleian Library, MS. Add. 186.

The Life of Sir Thomas Bodley, written by Himselfe Harleian Miscellany (London, 1745), 300–305 (the 1647 text).

The Life of Sir Thomas Bodley, written by Himselfe (Edinburgh, 1894). Privately printed for John Lane and his friends.

R. S. Granniss (ed.), *The Life of Sir Thomas Bodley, written by himself. Together with the first draft of the statues of the public library at Oxon* (Chicago, 1906).

Repr. Scarecrow (Metuchen, NJ, 1967).

Trencentale Bodleianum; a memorial volume for the three hundredth anniversary of the public funeral of Sir Thomas Bodley, March 29, 1613 (Oxford, 1913), 1–26.

The Life of Sir Thomas Bodley, written by Himselfe, facsimile (Oxford, 1983).